FAMOUS ARTISTS

MONET

The author, Antony Mason, is a freelance editor and author of
many books for children.

Designer	Tessa Barwick
Editor	Jen Green
Picture research	Brooks Krikler Research
Illustrators	Michaela Stewart
	Tessa Barwick

First edition for the United States, Canada, and the Philippines
published 1995 by Barron's Educational Series, Inc.

Designed and produced by
Aladdin Books Ltd
28 Percy Street
London W1P 9FF

First published in
Great Britain in 1994 by
Watts Books
96 Leonard Street
London EC2A 4RH

All inquiries should be addressed to:
Barron's Educational Series, Inc.
250 Wireless Boulevard
Hauppauge, New York 11788

Library of Congress Catalog Card No.: 94-22455

Mason, Antony.
Monet / Antony Mason. –1st U.S. ed.
p. cm.–(Famous artists)
"First published in Great Britain in 1994 by Watts Books" T.p. verso.
Includes index.
ISBN 0-8120-6494-1 (hardcover).–ISBN 0-8120-9174-4 (pbk.).
1. Monet, Claude, 1840-1926–Juvenile literature. 2. Painters–France–Biography–Juvenile
literature. 3. Art appreciation–Juvenile literature. [1. Monet, Claude, 1840-1926.
2. Artists. 3. Painting, French. 4. Art appreciation.] I. Monet,
Claude, 1840-1926. II. Title. III. Series.
ND553.M7M29   1995
759.4–dc20
94-22455
CIP   AC

International Standard Book No. 0-8120-6494-1 (hardcover)
0-8120-9174-4 (paperback)

Printed in Belgium
4567 4208 987654321

MONET

ANTONY MASON

BARRON'S

Contents

 The Artist's Garden at Giverny, painted in 1900.

INTRODUCTION

Claude Monet (1840-1926) is one of the most famous French artists in the history of modern painting. As a young man he rebelled against the traditional painting methods of his day. Monet wanted to paint pictures that captured the mood of his surroundings. Other young artists shared his ideas. Together they became known as the Impressionists. After years of struggle and poverty, Impressionism caught on and became one of the most important stepping stones in modern art. This book explores Monet's development from his childhood, when he drew clever sketches of his schoolteachers, to his old age as one of the most celebrated painters in France. The techniques he used are discussed, and you can try some of them for yourself. Below you can see how the book is organized.

The size of the paintings is indicated by these symbols.

About the artist's work at the time

Illustration of the artist's home or environment

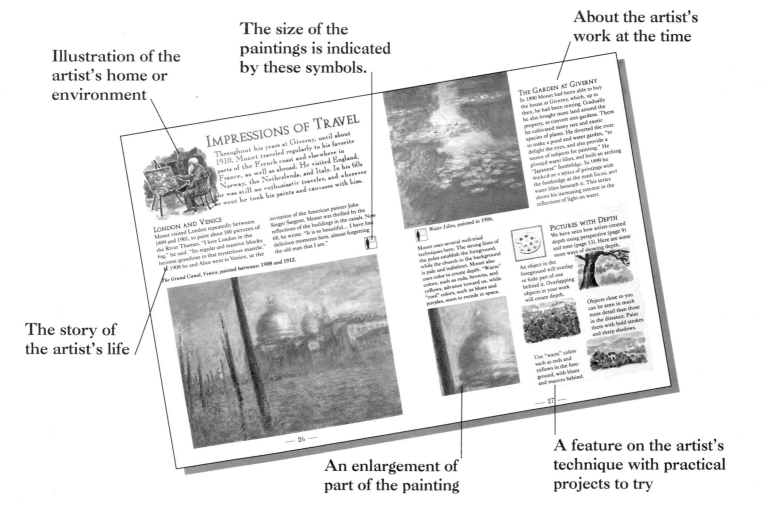

IMPRESSIONS OF TRAVEL

Throughout his years at Giverny, until about 1910, Monet traveled regularly to his favorite parts of the French coast and elsewhere in France, as well as abroad. He visited England, Norway, the Netherlands, and Italy. In his 60s he was still an enthusiastic traveler, and wherever he went he took his paints and canvases with him.

LONDON AND VENICE

Monet visited London repeatedly between 1899 and 1901, to paint about 100 pictures of the River Thames. "I love London in the fog," he said. "Its regular and massive blocks become grandiose in that mysterious mantle." In 1908 he and Alice went to Venice, at the

invitation of the American painter John Singer Sargent. Monet was thrilled by the reflections of the buildings in the canals. Now 68, he wrote: "It is so beautiful.... I have had delicious moments here, almost forgetting the old man that I am."

The Grand Canal, Venice, painted between 1908 and 1912.

Water Lilies, painted in 1906.

Monet uses several well-tried techniques here. The strong lines of the poles establish the foreground, while the church in the background is pale and indistinct. Monet also uses color to create depth. "Warm" colors, such as reds, browns, and yellows, advance toward us, while "cool" colors, such as blues and purples, seem to recede in space.

THE GARDEN AT GIVERNY

In 1890 Monet had been able to buy the house at Giverny, which, up to then, he had been renting. Gradually he also bought more land around the property, to convert into gardens. There he cultivated many rare and exotic species of plants. He diverted the river to make a pond and water garden, "to delight the eyes, and also provide a source of subjects for painting." He planted water lilies, and built an arching "Japanese" footbridge. In 1899 he worked on a series of paintings with the footbridge as the main focus, and water lilies beneath it. This series shows his increasing interest in the reflections of light on water.

PICTURES WITH DEPTH

We have seen how artists created depth using perspective (page 9) and tone (page 13). Here are some more ways of showing depth.

An object in the foreground will overlap or hide part of one behind it. Overlapping objects in your work will create depth.

Objects close to you can be seen in much more detail than those in the distance. Paint them with bold strokes and sharp shadows.

Use "warm" colors such as reds and yellows in the foreground, with blues and mauves behind.

— 26 —

— 27 —

The story of the artist's life

An enlargement of part of the painting

A feature on the artist's technique with practical projects to try

BOYHOOD BY THE SEA

Monet's talent as an artist showed itself from an early age. As a boy he drew caricatures of his teachers and friends, and even sold them. In his hometown of Le Havre, he met an artist who painted landscapes out-of-doors. Monet realized that this was what interested him most. As a teenager, the course of his life was set.

SCHOOL DAYS IN LE HAVRE

Claude Monet was born in Paris in November 1840. His father, Adolphe Monet, was a grocer, and the family lived in a flat over the shop. When Claude was about 6 years old his family moved to Le Havre, a port in Normandy in northern France (shown above). Here his father ran another grocery store, and Claude attended the local school.

Claude was a lively boy, with striking dark eyes and thick, dark hair. Schoolwork bored him, but he was popular at school, partly because of his talent for drawing witty caricatures of friends and teachers. Drawing was his great love, and he would often take a sketchbook down to the port to draw the fishermen and their boats in the harbor. His art teacher at school was a gifted painter. He gave Claude plenty of encouragement. Soon the boy found he could sell his drawings through a local art shop for a good price.

Claude's mother died in 1857, when he was 16. His family went to stay with his aunt, Marie-Jeanne Lecadre, who also lived in Le Havre. She was also a painter and knew some of the local artists. One of these was Eugène Boudin (1828-98). Boudin was considered unusual because he insisted on painting in the open air.

Boudin invited the young Monet to join him on his expeditions, and Claude was enthralled. "I understood, I saw, what painting could be!" he wrote. "From that moment on, my way was clear, my destiny decreed. I would be a painter, no matter what."

Monet drew these caricatures of his teachers and the people of Le Havre as a schoolboy.

BECOMING AN ARTIST

In the mid-nineteenth century, as today, it was hard to make a living as an artist. Claude's father Adolphe Monet was a practical man who foresaw the problems of pursuing such a career. He knew his son's friend, Eugène Boudin, was desperately poor.

In 1858 a painting by Claude was accepted for an exhibition organized by the city of Le Havre. This convinced the young artist that he had enough talent to become a professional painter. All the most important art schools were in Paris, and so, despite grave reservations voiced by his father, Claude decided to go there. He was now 18.

Claude attended the Académie Suisse in Paris, a relaxed and informal art school. Here he began a long friendship with the painter Camille Pissarro (1830-1903). In 1861, however, he had to sign on for military service and was sent with the army to Algeria in North Africa. The next year he contracted typhoid, a dangerous disease, and had to return to Le Havre. Now he met another influential friend, the Dutch painter Johan Barthold Jongkind (1819-91). The two artists went on outdoor painting trips. By the summer of 1862 Monet had decided not to return to Algeria but to go back to Paris, to study at the studio of a famous art teacher, Charles Gleyre.

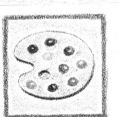

CARICATURES

Monet's caricatures were popular with his friends. In a caricature the features are exaggerated; the trick is to make the caricature look like a real person – someone that people can recognize. Try this yourself. First get to know the face of your subject by making an accurate sketch. Which are your subject's most obvious features? Now try a caricature, exaggerating the length of the nose or chin or the shape of the hairline. Monet used another tradition of caricature – putting the head on a tiny body. You could try this, too.

YOUNG ARTISTS IN PARIS

Charles Gleyre was a talented but old-fashioned painter. His pupils learned from him but were soon developing their own ideas. Monet made friends with a number of fellow pupils who became important influences in his life. These included Pierre-Auguste Renoir (1841-1919), Alfred Sisley (1839-99), and a wealthy young man named Frédéric Bazille (1841-70).

EARLY SUCCESS

Gleyre became ill and closed his studio in 1864, and Monet went back to Le Havre. At 24, he was poor but contented. In 1865 two of his seascapes were shown at the famous annual art exhibition in Paris called the Salon – a major achievement for a young painter.

The success encouraged Claude to attempt a huge outdoor project for the next year's Salon. It was a picnic scene, full of sunlight and dappled shadow, but Monet could not complete the painting. He ran out of money and had to abandon it.

Fragment from *The Picnic*, which Monet painted in 1865-66.

Although painting from real life, Monet composed his pictures carefully. The human figures here draw the viewer's eye into the painting, and help create depth.

 A street scene in Honfleur, a port near Le Havre. Monet painted several versions of this view in 1864.

A LACK OF FINISH

Monet's main interest was always outdoor scenes. Working with Boudin and Jongkind had helped him to appreciate the effects of sunlight. He found that to reproduce the mood and light of a sunny day, he had to work rapidly. The fashionable paintings of the day were quite different; they were usually carefully painted scenes from history. Compared to these, Monet's works seemed hurried; critics said they looked unfinished.

PERSPECTIVE

Artists give their work a sense of depth by using perspective. Perspective relies on the fact that objects look smaller the further away they are. Lines that in real life run parallel, such as the roofs of houses on opposite sides of a street, appear to converge and meet at a point in the distance, known as the vanishing point. Experiment with perspective by drawing a vanishing point first, with straight lines radiating from it like spokes from a wheel. Now base a street scene on this pattern.

CAMILLE

Monet failed to finish his picnic scene, but he was determined to submit a painting to the Salon of 1866. Back in Paris, he produced a picture called "The Woman in the Green Dress." It was accepted by the Salon, and was a huge success. For this painting he used the model who appeared in "The Picnic," Camille Doncieux.

LOVE AND MONEY

Monet fell in love with Camille, and soon they were living together. She was 19 years old, the daughter of a wealthy merchant. When Adolphe Monet found out about the relationship he was furious. In those days it was a scandal for unmarried partners to live together. Adolphe stopped the regular allowance on which his son depended, and refused to meet Camille. Claude and Camille moved to the town of Sèvres on the Seine outside Paris, and then to Le Havre. They were very poor. Monet could barely afford to buy painting materials but was helped by his friend Bazille and by his aunt.

Terrace at Sainte-Adresse, 1866, shows Monet's father seated, probably beside his aunt.

In *Women in the Garden* Monet experimented with sunlight and shade. The painting includes a study of a hand and a bunch of flowers in sunlight (left) and in shadow.

 The figures in *Women in the Garden* (1866-67) are almost life-size.

PAINTING IN THE OPEN AIR

While living at Sèvres, Monet worked on another large and ambitious project. This was a painting featuring Camille in four different poses, dappled with sunlight.

Monet was determined to paint the whole of this work outside, in the garden – not in a studio as most artists of the time would have done. The canvas was so big that he dug a trench and placed the base in it, so that he could paint the upper part of the picture.

Women in the Garden was rejected by the Paris Salon of 1867, much to Monet's disappointment. Bazille, distressed at Monet's poverty, decided to buy the painting from him. He paid the handsome sum of 2,500 francs, which he gave to Monet in monthly installments.

USING COLOR

The relationship between colors is demonstrated by the color wheel shown here. The purest colors – red, yellow, and blue – are known as the primary colors. The secondary colors, orange, green, and purple, can be mixed from the primaries on either side. Monet could mix even very dark colors from the primaries.

Try mixing the secondary colors from the primaries yourself. Then paint a picture using as many colors as you can make from just the primaries.

FLIGHT FROM WAR

Adolphe Monet still refused to see Camille, even when his son was living with her in Le Havre. In 1867 Adolphe insisted that the couple should part. Claude sent Camille to Paris but continued to see her. In August she gave birth to their first son, Jean, and Claude moved back to Paris to live with them.

OUTBREAK OF WAR

Claude and Camille stayed in Paris until money problems forced them to return to Le Havre. They spent happy days there as a young family. Monet continued to paint energetically, and he even managed to sell a few pictures.

By 1869 they were back in Paris. During the summer, Monet joined his friend Pierre-Auguste Renoir on painting expeditions. Together they visited a popular gathering place on the River Seine called La Grenouillère. There they concentrated on reproducing the effects of light on water.

The following year, 1870, Monet married Camille. But France was suddenly thrown into chaos when its Emperor, Napoleon III, declared war on the powerful German state of Prussia. Like many other people, Monet left France, with Camille and Jean, in order to avoid being called upon to fight. They went to London (above left), where they lived for nine months. During Monet's stay in Britain, his father died. This death was closely followed by that of his aunt. News reached him, too, that his loyal friend Bazille had been killed in battle.

When the war ended, Monet and Camille traveled to the Netherlands. In 1871 they returned to France to set up home in Argenteuil, a small town on the Seine on the outskirts of Paris.

Bathers at La Grenouillère, 1869. **Monet's paintings of this subject were rejected by the Paris Salon.**

Monet painted *The Thames below Westminster* in 1871, during his stay in Britain.

Figures or objects seen against the light appear as dark outlines, called silhouettes. The silhouetted figures here are not painted in detail but contribute to the mood of the scene.

IMAGES OF LONDON

Monet continued to paint while he was in exile, as did his friend Pissarro, who was in London at the same time. Monet applied the techniques that he had developed in the previous months with Renoir to capture the shimmering effect of light on the River Thames. He learned to find beauty in the misty landscapes of a big city.

DEPTH AND TONE

You have seen how objects appear smaller the further away they are (page 9). They also become lighter in color. You can experiment with this effect by painting a landscape using different tones, or shades, of color. First paint a pale sky. On top of the sky paint the most distant part of the landscape in a light gray color. Then use a darker shade of gray to paint the foreground nearest to the viewer. By using progressively lighter tones in the distance, you will create the illusion of depth.

IMPRESSIONISM IS BORN

In London Monet had met an art dealer named Paul Durand-Ruel. In 1872 Durand-Ruel returned to Paris and began to sell Monet's paintings quite successfully. But Monet and the artists in his circle were rejected by the Paris Salons. In response, in 1874 Monet and his friends decided to hold an exhibition of their own.

FIRST IMPRESSIONIST EXHIBITION

The exhibition presented works by many artists who are now world famous, including Renoir, Pissarro, and Sisley. At the time, however, it was not a success. A few critics admired the new style, but most ridiculed what the artists were trying to do. Among the paintings was a work by Monet called *Impression: Sunrise*. A critic seized on this and mockingly called the artists "Impressionists." The group liked the name. That is how Impressionism, one of the great movements in Western art, got its name.

Impression: Sunrise, 1872. **Monet captured the harbor with a few quick lines.**

The bank of poppies, painted in bright, unmixed color, gives this painting its peculiar charm. If the details had been given a more finished look, the impression of movement and heat would have been lost.

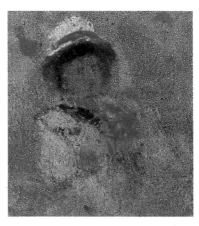

Poppy Field, 1873, shows Camille and Jean near Argenteuil.

PEACE AND BEAUTY

Monet and Camille enjoyed happy, relaxed days at Argenteuil. Now in his early 30s, Monet produced some of his most charming work, reflecting his contentment. His colors became lighter, and his compositions braver. Like his fellow Impressionists, he had become a master of atmosphere, intent on capturing the mood of a landscape as it might be only at that particular hour, in those particular weather conditions.

IMPRESSIONIST ART

With a set of bright poster paints or watercolors, you too can paint like an Impressionist. Work from a photograph, or in the open air, as Monet did. Try to keep your paints clear and clean as you work and do not let your colors become muddy. Work quickly; like the Impressionists, you are trying to convey the general mood of what you see, not to produce a detailed image. Use small, rapid brushstrokes, even when painting quite large shapes. Place strokes of different colors close to each other to give the impression of shimmering light.

Patronage and Poverty

The Impressionists held a series of further exhibitions in the coming years, but none was successful, and they all had to struggle to survive. In 1876 Monet found a wealthy patron to support him, an art collector named Ernest Hoschedé, and for a few years he lived more comfortably. But in 1878 disaster struck.

Hard Times

Ernest Hoschedé was a passionate admirer of art. With his support, Monet was able to pursue projects that interested him, such as his studies of Gare Saint-Lazare, a railway station in Paris. In 1878, however, Ernest Hoschedé lost all his money. Camille gave birth to a second son, Michel, in March, but now they faced real poverty. The Monets moved to a cheaper house at Vétheuil on the Seine. There, to add to their burden, they were joined by the entire Hoschedé family, including their six children.

Monet continued to paint, often using his studio boat (above) on the river. He received some financial help from more wealthy artists, but was close to despair. During the winter of 1878-79 his family was cold and hungry. Camille became ill, and Monet could not afford medicines.

Camille's health worsened through 1879. She was nursed tenderly by Ernest Hoschedé's wife, Alice, but died in September. Now 38, Monet confessed: "I am filled with dismay to find myself alone with my poor children."

The cheerful, holiday atmosphere of *Rue Montorgueil Decked Out with Flags* contrasts with Monet's grim circumstances in 1878.

The writer Emile Zola praised Monet's railway scenes: "One can hear the rumbling of the trains, and see the smoke rolling through the huge sheds. Here is the painting of today, these beautiful, broad, modern canvases."

The Gare Saint-Lazare, painted in 1877.

STEAM POWER

Monet painted a series of twelve studies of Gare Saint-Lazare, a vivid response to the sights of the Industrial Age, and a new direction for his work. These are robust portraits of the world of steam power – noisy, dirty, and busy, but also exciting. Monet proved that Impressionist methods could be applied to urban subjects.

PAINTING INDUSTRY

Not all paintings have to be of conventionally beautiful scenery; bustling city streets and even factory scenes can also have great energy and power. Try an urban landscape yourself using pastels or wax crayons, which are good for portraying smoke and haze. You could draw a chimney belching white smoke into a dark sky. Add touches of color to the smoke, then blend the colors together with your finger to create a smudged effect.

The Comfort of Alice

Staying on at Vétheuil (right) after the death of Camille, Monet remained depressed and barely able to paint. The reassuring presence of Alice Hoschedé brought him comfort. Gradually, in the early 1880s, Monet's paintings began to meet with success, and meanwhile his love for Alice grew. This was a turning point in Monet's life.

The Artist's Garden at Vétheuil, painted in 1880. Monet was an enthusiastic gardener. The artist often used figures (usually members of his family) as a focus in his compositions.

Seascapes and Scandal

The Impressionists held their fourth exhibition in 1879, but Monet was too exhausted to make any great contribution to it. From now on he became less closely associated with the movement.

In 1880, however, a magazine called *La Vie Moderne* offered to put on a one-man show of his work. During an interview for the show, he was asked where his studio was. He replied with a sweeping gesture across the landscape of the River Seine: "This is my studio!" As the map on page 10 shows, Monet spent most of his life by this great river, which was a constant inspiration for his work.

The art dealer Paul Durand-Ruel believed that Monet's pictures of the sea and coast could become popular. In 1881 he sent the artist to paint at Etretat (near Le Havre). Suddenly Monet's paintings began to sell well.

In December he moved from Vétheuil to Poissy, still on the Seine but closer to Paris. Much to the disapproval of neighbors and friends, Alice now left her husband to join Monet there, with her children – then a very shocking thing for a married woman to do.

The Banks of the Seine at Bougival, 1880, shows ice blocks floating downriver in the thaw.

BITTER WINTERS

During 1878-80 northern France suffered two particularly cold winters. To Monet, however, the snow and ice provided a new challenge: to capture the winter light and somber tones of the landscape – even though this meant spending long hours in freezing temperatures. The desolate quality of these landscapes seems to reflect the artist's own mood.

SNOW AND FROST

Painting a winter scene will be easy if you follow the tips shown here. To paint flakes of falling snow, you will need a white candle. Use the end of the candle to make wax dots on your paper. The dots will resist a wash of paint laid on top, to form snowflakes. Bare winter trees can be created by using a dry paintbrush to lift out the outlines of branches while the background is still wet. The effect of frost on grass can be achieved by scraping the paper with the edge of a craft knife once the paint is completely dry.

GIVERNY

In the spring of 1883 Monet set out to look for a new home where he could live with Alice and their large combined family of eight children. He found an old farmhouse in the north of France, on the junction of the River Epte and the Seine. The village was called Giverny, and it was to be his beloved home for over 40 years.

THE PERFECT HOME

When Monet first saw Giverny (above), the orchards were full of blossoms. Ranks of poplar trees cast long shadows in the water, and the scene was framed by gentle hills. It was the perfect Impressionist landscape. "Once settled, I hope to produce masterpieces, because the countryside here pleases me very much," Monet wrote to Paul Durand-Ruel, who paid for the move.

The artist immediately set to work developing the garden, which became a passionate interest. He used a large barn as a studio, and brought his four boats, including the old studio boat, to the River Epte.

These were happy and productive years. Monet worked feverishly, setting out early in the morning or in the evening, to make the most of the light at dawn and dusk.

He returned regularly to the coast at Etretat. In 1886 he visited the island of Belle-Ile, off the coast of Brittany. An art critic who met him there described him as "a rough man, tanned, bearded, wearing heavy boots, dressed in coarse material, a sailor's beret on his head, a wooden pipe projecting from his thick beard, and in the center of all that, a fine profile and an intelligent eye."

Woman with a Parasol had been one of Monet's favorite subjects when Camille was alive. This version was painted in 1886.

Monet produced some of his finest seascapes on the island of Belle-Ile. He used short, broken brushstrokes to capture the restless power of the sea surging around the jagged rocks beneath a sunless sky.

Rocks at Belle-Ile, one of 10 cliff scenes painted in 1886.

THE RAGING SEA

Rugged coastal landscapes held a great attraction for Monet, and he would take unusual risks to paint the view from a particular angle. In 1881, working in a terrible storm at Etretat with his easel tied to the cliff, he was washed off the rocks and nearly drowned. He painted in all weather and his hardiness was legendary – as was his bad temper if the weather changed while he was working on a picture.

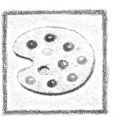

PAINTING WATER

Water is transparent. What we see, when we look at a still pond or a slow-moving river, are mainly reflections of the sky and the landscape. When water moves, in waves or in ripples, these reflections are reshaped into patterns or broken into tiny pieces. Take time to study water carefully before you paint it. You will often find that reflections contain more colors and images than you expect. Try to reproduce these as accurately as you can. You'll be surprised at the result!

THE SERIES PAINTINGS

In 1891 Ernest Hoschedé died, and the following year Monet married Alice. At about this time his painting became simpler and began to depend more on color alone for its impact. Monet had always been interested in the effects of light. Now he took this one step further by making a series of paintings of the same subject in different light conditions.

HAYSTACKS AND POPLARS

Monet chose the haystacks standing in the fields around his house as the subject of his first large series. Earlier in his life he had often painted more than one picture of the same subject. But now he was studying the effects of light at different times of day, or in different seasons, in an almost scientific way. His idea was that all the paintings should be exhibited together so that the viewer could see the changes in light that had taken place over time.

In 1891 he showed 15 of his *Haystacks* series at the Durand-Ruel Gallery, and they were a great success. The same year he worked on another series, this time of the poplar trees lining the river near Giverny.

Haystacks at Giverny, one of a series painted in 1890 and 1891.

ONE VIEW, MANY PICTURES

The *Haystacks* series began one day when Monet noticed that the light had changed while he was painting. Instead of altering the painting itself, Monet asked one of his stepdaughters to fetch another canvas, so he could represent this changed light. As the day progressed, he asked for another canvas, then another. He also returned to the subject at various times of year.

Poplars, one of a series painted in 1891.

 *Haystacks at Sunset, Frosty Weather,* 1890-91.

Monet painted quickly. One visitor described the process: "Once in front of his easel, he draws in a few lines with the charcoal and then attacks the painting directly, handling his long brushes with an astounding agility and sure sense of design.... His landscape is swiftly set down and could, if necessary, be considered complete after barely an hour and often much less."

COMPLEMENTARIES

In his *Haystacks* series, Monet often painted haystacks and their shadows in contrasting, or *complementary*, colors. If you look at the color wheel on page 11, you will see that each of the primary colors has a secondary color opposite it. For example, green is opposite, or complementary, to red. Many artists believe the shadow of an object is best represented by its complementary color. Test this theory for yourself, with a subject such as fruit.

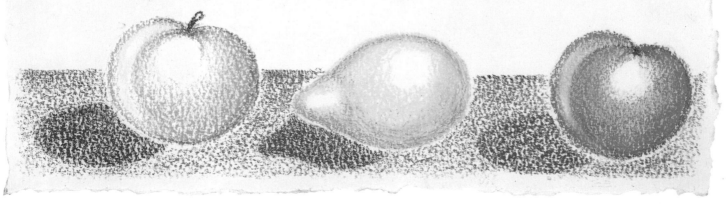

CAPTURING THE LIGHT

Throughout his 50s, Monet continued to work at Giverny. By this time he and other Impressionist artists were famous, and their paintings sold for high prices. Giverny received a series of visitors, artists, and critics from France and abroad. Monet loved to show them his garden, which he had been developing since he moved there.

ROUEN CATHEDRAL

In 1892 Monet went to Rouen, a city on the Seine near Giverny, and began a series of 18 paintings of the front of the cathedral. He aimed to show the play of light on the intricate stonework at different times of day.

Rouen Cathedral **bathed in early morning light, 1892-93.**

Rouen Cathedral in Full Sunlight, **painted in 1892-93.**

Monet's visitors at Giverny were not allowed to interrupt his work. The artist worked intensely and sometimes flew into rages if his painting did not go well. At such times even his family kept out of his way and waited until his fury had passed.

STUDIO WORK

To get the view he wanted, Monet painted Rouen Cathedral from a second-floor room above a shop. Later, back at Giverny, he did more work on the pictures in his studio. He had always insisted on painting in the open air, and so at first he was reluctant to admit that he sometimes reworked his paintings in the studio. But as he grew older he did more and more work indoors.

The series paintings were exhibited together as Monet had intended, and were acclaimed by the critics. One believed they marked "the beginning of a new age in our history of sensation and expression." The artist's subject had become the passage of time itself.

Rouen Cathedral at Sunset, **1892-93.**

CHANGING LIGHT

Every view changes according to the weather and time of day. Look at a garden, or your school playground. In the early morning it might look bluish-gray, tinged with pink. As the sun rises higher, the colors will become stronger and shapes more distinct. In the evening, shadows lengthen, and colors and shapes soften and may turn golden. Try doing a series of paintings of the same scene to show how different it can look at various times of the day or year.

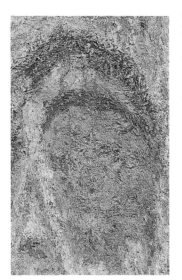

Monet portrayed the basic structure of the cathedral accurately, but the details of the stonework have been left vague. Instead, he concentrated on the effect of light, producing more than 40 versions of this subject in 1892 and 1893.

IMPRESSIONS OF TRAVEL

Throughout his years at Giverny, until about 1910, Monet traveled regularly to his favorite parts of the French coast and elsewhere in France, as well as abroad. He visited England, Norway, the Netherlands, and Italy. In his 60s he was still an enthusiastic traveler, and wherever he went he took his paints and canvases with him.

LONDON AND VENICE

Monet visited London repeatedly between 1899 and 1901, to paint about 100 pictures of the River Thames. "I love London in the fog," he said. "Its regular and massive blocks become grandiose in that mysterious mantle."

In 1908 he and Alice went to Venice, at the invitation of the American painter John Singer Sargent. Monet was thrilled by the reflections of the buildings in the canals. Now 68, he wrote: "It is so beautiful.... I have had delicious moments here, almost forgetting the old man that I am."

The Grand Canal, Venice, **painted between 1908 and 1912.**

THE GARDEN AT GIVERNY

In 1890 Monet had been able to buy the house at Giverny, which, up to then, he had been renting. Gradually he also bought more land around the property, to convert into gardens. There he cultivated many rare and exotic species of plants. He diverted the river to make a pond and water garden, "to delight the eyes, and also provide a source of subjects for painting." He planted water lilies, and built an arching "Japanese" footbridge. In 1899 he worked on a series of paintings with the footbridge as the main focus, and water lilies beneath it. This series shows his increasing interest in the reflections of light on water.

 Water Lilies, painted in 1906.

Monet uses several well-tried techniques here. The strong lines of the poles establish the foreground, while the church in the background is pale and indistinct. Monet also uses color to create depth. "Warm" colors, such as reds, browns, and yellows, advance toward us, while "cool" colors, such as blues and purples, seem to recede in space.

PICTURES WITH DEPTH

We have seen how artists created depth using perspective (page 9) and tone (page 13). Here are some more ways of showing depth.

An object in the foreground will overlap or hide part of one behind it. Overlapping objects in your work will create depth.

Objects close to you can be seen in much more detail than those in the distance. Paint them with bold strokes and sharp shadows.

Use "warm" colors such as reds and yellows in the foreground, with blues and mauves behind.

FINAL YEARS

In 1911 Monet's beloved wife, Alice, died after a long illness. Monet was distraught, and cut himself off from the world for many months. By now his eyesight was failing, and he could not see colors properly. In 1914 his son Jean died. These were difficult years, yet Monet still produced some of his most beautiful, original work.

WATER LILIES

Towards the end of his life Monet hardly left his home at Giverny. The gardens and the pond he had designed and planted became the inspiration for all his work.

Monet had renewed his old friendship with Georges Clemenceau, a politician. In 1918 Clemenceau became Prime Minister of France. He persuaded the artist to begin work on a series of enormous water lily paintings. This was a project that dominated Monet's painting for the rest of his life. The artist had a large studio built at Giverny so that he could surround himself with the vast canvases.

During his last years Monet's health suffered. His eyes were dimmed by cataracts – opaque layers that form over the lens of the eye. His sense of color was affected, though he carried on with his work. For a long while he refused to have an operation to remove the cataracts, fearing that he would lose his eyesight altogether. But in 1923 the operation was successful and his vision improved greatly. At the age of 83, he reported, "I have my sight back at last, to my great joy, and have worked all summer with more zeal than ever." But by 1926 he was suffering from lung cancer (he had always been a heavy smoker). In his last illness he was nursed by Blanche Hoschedé, his stepdaughter and the widow of his son Jean. In December 1926, at the age of 86, he died, with Clemenceau at his side. He was buried with simple ceremony at Giverny.

The Clouds, 1918-26. These studies of flowers and reflections come close to abstract art.

Agapanthus, 1914-17, a flower study painted when Monet's eyesight was poor.

After Monet's death, a series of water lily paintings was placed in a special gallery in Paris. They display a new, almost abstract vision, and were much admired by later artists. Through them Monet shows himself a pioneer of twentieth-century art, as he had been of Impressionism so many years before.

ABSTRACT ART
Abstract paintings rely for effect on patterns, shapes, or swirls of paint; they do not try to portray the real world. During Monet's lifetime, artists began to see that abstract art could have great power. Try an abstract painting. Cover your paper with swirls of paint, allowing colors to blend while they are wet. You might want to use your abstract design as the basis of a different kind of painting, of a cloudy landscape (below) or a stormy sea.

CHRONOLOGY OF MONET'S LIFE

1840 Born in Paris, France.
1846 Family moved to Le Havre, in northern France.
1859 Went to Paris and trained at the Académie Suisse; met Pissarro.
1861-62 Military service in Algeria, during which he caught typhoid.
1862 Began studies at the studio of Charles Gleyre. Met Renoir and Sisley.
1865-66 Painted *The Picnic*, using Camille Doncieux as his model.
1867 Camille gave birth to their first child, Jean.
1870 Monet married Camille. They fled to London at the outbreak of the Franco-Prussian War.
1871 They returned to France, and set up home at Argenteuil.
1874 An exhibition by Monet, Renoir, Sisley, Pissarro, and others gave them the title "Impressionists."
1876 Ernest Hoschedé, a wealthy patron, commissioned Monet.
1878 A second son, Michel, was born. Camille was now very ill, and Monet was penniless. They moved to Vétheuil.
1879 Death of Camille.
1881 Monet moved to Poissy, and was joined by Alice Hoschedé.
1883 Monet and Alice, with their eight children, moved to Giverny.
1890-91 Monet painted the *Haystacks* series, the first of his series paintings.
1911 Death of Alice.
1914-26 Painted the *Water Lily* series.
1926 Monet died at Giverny at the age of 86.

A BRIEF HISTORY OF ART

The world's earliest works of art are figurines dating from 30,000 B.C. Cave art developed from 16,000 B.C. In the Classical Age (500-400 B.C.) sculpture flourished in Ancient Greece.

The Renaissance period began in Italy in the 1300s and reached its height in the sixteenth century. Famous Italian artists include Giotto (ca. 1266-1337), Leonardo da Vinci (1452-1519), Michelangelo Buonarroti (1475-1564), and Titian (ca. 1487-1576).

In Europe during the fifteenth and sixteenth centuries, Hieronymus Bosch (active 1480-1516), Albrecht Dürer (1471-1528), Pieter Breughel the Elder (1525-69), and El Greco (1541-1614) produced great art. Artists of the Baroque period include Peter Paul Rubens (1577-1640) and Rembrandt van Rijn (1606-69).

During the Romantic movement, English artists J.M.W. Turner (1775-1851) and John Constable (1776-1837) produced wonderful landscapes. Francisco Goya (1746-1828) was a great Spanish portrait artist.

Impressionism began in France in the 1870s. Artists include **Claude Monet** (1840-1926), Camille Pissarro (1830-1903), and Edgar Degas (1834-1917). Post-Impressionists include Paul Cézanne (1839-1906), Paul Gauguin (1848-1903), and Vincent Van Gogh (1853-90).

The twentieth century has seen many movements in art. Georges Braque (1882-1963) painted in the Cubist tradition, Salvador Dali (1904-89) in the Surrealist. Pablo Picasso (1881-1973) was a prolific Spanish painter. More recently Jackson Pollock (1912-56) and David Hockney (1937-) have achieved fame.

Museums and Galleries

The following museums and galleries have examples of Monet's work:

The Louvre, Paris, France

The Orangerie, Paris, France

Musée d'Orsay, Paris, France

Musée Marmottan, Paris, France

Metropolitan Museum of Art, New York

National Gallery of Art, Washington, D.C.

Museum of Fine Arts, Boston, Massachusetts

Philadelphia Museum of Art, Pennsylvania

Art Institute of Chicago, Illinois

Fogg Art Museum, Harvard, Cambridge, Massachusetts

National Gallery, London, England

Tate Gallery, London, England

National Gallery of Australia, Canberra

Pushkin Museum, Moscow, Russia

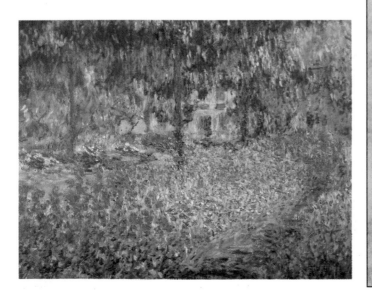

Glossary

Abstract art Some paintings consist only of patterns and colors; they do not attempt to depict things in the real world, such as people, houses, or landscapes. Such paintings are referred to as abstract art.

Caricature A humorous portrait of someone, with the facial features deliberately exaggerated.

Complementary colors A system that divides contrasting colors into opposites, as shown by the color wheel. Each primary color has an opposing secondary color; for example, the complementary color of red is green.

Depth Paintings are made on flat surfaces, but artists can give the impression of distance through the use of color and perspective. This illusion of distance is called *depth*.

Impressionism An art movement that began in Paris in the 1870s. Impressionist painters attempted to portray the light and mood of a scene by using bright colors and small, rapid brushstrokes. The term "Impressionist" was first used in 1874. The main Impressionist painters were Monet, Renoir, Pissarro, and Sisley, but there were many others who were associated with them or who painted in their style.

Perspective Since the fifteenth century, artists have used perspective to suggest distance in their paintings. Objects usually look smaller the further away they are.

Studio The building or room in which an artist works. Purpose-built studios are usually spacious rooms, with large windows to let in plenty of light, but not direct sunlight.

INDEX

INDEX OF PICTURES

PICTURE CREDITS:
Special thanks to: The Bridgeman Art Library; Giraudon/ Bridgeman Art Library; Musée Marmottan, Paris; Bequest of John T. Spaulding, Museum of Fine Arts, Boston; Frank Spooner Pictures; Roger Vlitos. The publishers have made every effort to contact all the relevant copyright holders and apologize for any omissions that may have inadvertently been made.